CLEAR HER NAME

Clear Her Name

A Mother's Journey in Legal Research to Save Her Daughter

Anelia Sutton

IRON Sharpens IRON Council

CLEAR HER NAME: A MOTHER'S JOURNEY IN LEGAL RESEARCH TO SAVE HER DAUGHTER is a work of nonfiction.

Copyright © All rights reserved

In accordance with the U.S. Copyright Act of 1976, this book is licensed for your personal enjoyment only. No part of this publication may be reproduced without prior written permission of the publisher. While the publisher and author have used their best efforts in preparing this book, they make no representations or warranties with respect to the accuracy or completeness of the contents of this book and specifically disclaim any implied guarantees, warranties of merchantability or fitness for a particular purpose. The advice and strategies contained herein may not be suitable for you. You should consult with a professional where appropriate. Neither the publisher nor the author shall be liable for any profit or any other commercial damages, including but not limited to special, incidental, consequential, or other Damages. Trademarks, service marks, product names or names featured in this publication are assumed the property of their owners and are used as reference only. The publisher and author do not give medical or legal advice. Although the information contained in this book provides preventative steps to increase your knowledge of self-governance, there are no guarantees.

Clear her name: a mother's journey in legal research to save her daughter / anelia sutton
1. Law, research 2. Activism, global.
sutton, anelia, 1968-

© 2021 anelia sutton

Imprint
Iron Sharpens Iron Council is a division of Joy 55 Trust. Name and logo are trademarks of Joy 55 Trust. The publisher is not responsible for websites or their content that are not owned by the publisher.

Printed in the United States of America
Cover design by anelia sutton

Dedication

WITH LOVE to my family.

*WITH GRATITUDE to my daughter whose
wisdom restored my faith in humanity.*

*WITH HOPE to future generations whom I entrust my dream
of a kinder world.*

*WITH INTROSPECTION to the purveyors of lies and half-truths
- it's never too late to fix your heart!*

*Iron sharpens iron
So one man sharpens another*
Proverbs 27:17

DISCLAIMER

I am not a subject-matter expert on the content of this book. Therefore, not one thing should be construed as medical, financial, or legal advice whatsoever, omissions and errors excepted. I share my opinions which are intended for entertainment value. Any advice that I share is based purely on my personal experiences and is totally influenced by whatever mood I'm in whilst writing. Be advised to treat the content herein as a starting point that you shall mix into your melting pot of information whenever you make your decisions.

I have no idea why agents and gatekeepers do what they do. Time reveals all about them and their minions. Meanwhile, keep moving forward.

The purpose of this work is to share knowledge on how to farm - not how to pick a carrot. Use the information herein for the benefit of yourself and to uplift your community, not to rob them of the little they have.

Go forward. Go easy, but go.

CHAPTER ONE
"If you are silent about your pain, they'll kill you and say you enjoyed it."
- Zora Neale Hurston

SHELLSHOCK. Imagine taking prescription drugs that were legally prescribed to you, suffering from an adverse drug reaction from those prescription drugs causing you to become uncharacteristically deluded and violent, and being charged with committing a criminal offense during that state of delusion.

This happened to my daughter. My daughter went to the oral surgeon to have her wisdom teeth removed and ended up in jail. She was prescribed too many of the wrong medications, which led to a psychotic break.

I've taken on the difficult mission of spearheading the effort to clear my daughter's name, acting as its public face and a firsthand witness to the unjust treatment my daughter has received. By increasing awareness of the problem, creating both emotional and logical appeals and motivating others to help us convince those in power to do the right thing, we will seek to restore my daughter's rights, justify the battles I've been forced to engage in, and gain publicity and national awareness for an issue which — given the massive issue of over and mis-prescribing powerful medications that are only now being fully uncovered — is undoubtedly impacting many others across the country today.

My daughter has been unmistakably wronged by numerous parties, including the State of Virginia, prosecutors, her own attorneys, State doctors, and more. The most grievous of these wrongs being the theft of her children, and her freedom. Though there is clear evidence that she is perfectly capable of living a safe, normal life provided she is not prescribed mind-altering medications, she was imprisoned by a State psychiatric facility, forced to take medications, and denied the right to be a mother.

I'm sharing my story, not because I'm an exhibitionist or because my heart stopped hurting, but because I am a survivor. It's in my DNA. Through the years, I learned the power of forgiveness. And the truth is that I made a decision to own my story. It is why I made the decision to change my name on social media platforms from Anelia to Anne Smith to protect my daughter's desire for privacy. Years after her case was closed, I decided to use my birth name with my daughter's support, of course. By doing so, I open myself to move toward the healing I desire, and in that space of healing, in my own healing, I hope to help other people to heal too or at least to become open to heal their pain as well.

What I know for sure is the journey continues and I welcome all of it as a gift, be it a blessing or a lesson. And above all, I want everyone to realize that nobody is going to save us. We have to save ourselves. We are the change we need. One more thing. If you're uncomfortable about facts, or a truth and your reaction is to stick your head in the sand because it's too uncomfortable, this is going to be a bumpy ride for you. Facts should never upset you, they should enlighten you. So hold on to your fedora, it's going to be a bumpy ride. By the end of this short book, I'll present some solutions to overcoming the challenges we face in this crisis. One thing I know for sure is the people who are corrupt can dish it but they can't take it. It's time we put a stop to their shenanigans by exposing the truth about how to play the game and win. Beginning with this testimonial from a man who watched my videos for free on YouTube.

"Hear with Heart, not Ears. If you listen to the words with empathy, you'll hear the struggle and the history. Empathy is needed."
- Unknown

WHO SHOULD READ THIS BOOK. Transformation comes from transparency. This book is for you if you've ever wondered how and when we went from "innocent until proven guilty" to having to prove our innocence to be railroaded.

Railroaded: to convict with undue haste and by means of false charges or insufficient evidence.

I was knocked down to the floor when I received the phone call that my daughter and two grandchildren were in the hospital in Virginia. Shortly afterwards, I began taking care of my grandchildren in Maryland while their father reamined in Virginia to work when my daughter was arrested and charged with attempted murder. It was all happening so fast and it felt surreal.

Held in jail for 21 months waiting for a trial for a medical emergency. Doctors testified she was out of her mind. Her husband testified she was out of her mind and would never hurt their babies if she wasn't out of her mind. The verdict was Not Guilty by Reason of Insanity (NGRI), and she was committed to a state hospital with annual reviews. The annual reviews would go on for 5 years despite the facts about the case proving her innocence. She was railroaded.

I learned to be stronger from my daughter. The way that my daughter handled the ordeal made me stronger. Even in the midst of the worst storm and everyone around her inflicting their negative will onto her, she remained positive and handled it with grace. On the other hand, I did not -- everything that was happening to her was tearing me apart every day and some days it was difficult for me to breathe. Today, I'm able to take deep breaths by practicing the Wim Hof breathing method of meditation which is taking 30 deep breaths in the morning, which has done wonders for my physical health and mental health. Whenever I feel myself paying too much attention to the negativity going on in the world, I remind myself to focus on the things that I have to be grateful for.

I've grown spiritually during the most recent three years and I've become an ordained minister, but my belief isn't found in organized religion. My belief is simple: make decisions based on love and a close second is to help people, especially those who can't help themselves. But in a fame-obsessed world filled with clout chasers, people choose to help others for their own selfish gains. I accept everyone for who they are along with their journey in this thing called life. I am no longer bothered by what others choose to do when they choose to do evil things. I remind myself to "love the sinner, hate the sin". The truth is, most of the things we experience promote fear to keep us trapped in a cycle of negativity. Which is to say that we are more powerful than we were led to believe .

I'm FAR from perfect. I have faults and I make mistakes. But I'm not a quitter. I'm writing, researching and studying constantly. It is what's required to win the art of war. When the time comes, my dream is to retire to the back of the building lost in research as your trusted librarian. Until then I remain on front street doing what needs to be done. Mission Possible is my life and legacy. I owe it to myself, my progeny and to my brothers and sisters who are here fighting the good fight.

I light fires for the peaceful warriors who want to conquer public and private operations. It's blood, sweat and tears that would take 10,000 hours of full time research to master this sh*t, let alone write it up and serve it on a silver platter. None of it came easy. The untold sacrifices will never be known.

Innocent people's lives are destroyed based on contrived actions of egomaniacs who want a conviction, despite the obvious innocence. The legal system is rigged where justice is "pay to play" but my prayer is to wake the masses to how our legal system is using the media to spin propaganda to win, rather than seek justice. In fact, media propaganda is used effectively to convince the public of whatever narrative from any prosecutor where their actions are backed by the government with unlimited funds. I know this playbook all too well from personal experience because it is exactly what happened to my daughter, a young woman who is loved. By writing this book the world will know the truth, as well as her children, who are also victims of the prosecutor's scam.

For years, I was totally isolated and alone. Then I realized the only way I would shake it off was to find a deeper purpose for my life. Hundreds of years from now, my hope is that people will look back at these gross injustices and know the savage nature of the past world.

"Absolute power corrupts absolutely".
- Lord Acton

To be sure about the facts that form the foundation for this book, a young woman went to her orthodontist to have her wisdom teeth extracted. She experienced a severe drug reaction to psychoactive drugs that caused her to behave violently which is out of her normal character. She was arrested and waited in jail for 21 months for a trial. During this time, the officials across different departments -- including the CPS Virginia Beach employees and the Family Court, all worked in tandem with one another to operate from the position as if my daughter was guilty -- BEFORE -- her trial. Then when the verdict was Not Guilty by Reason of Insanity (NGRI), none of the agencies issued an apology. They were simply willing to allow the monster narrative to just be. After my daughter's verdict, she was escorted back to her jail cell to "wait for a bed in a state hospital" AFTER the verdict. This was shocking to me. How could this be? She's not guilty. That part is the criminal side. The verdict in a criminal trial should have concluded the criminal aspect. However, for the next 3 years, my daughter was escorted to the courthouse by the sheriff's department wearing shackles and handcuffs. This is wrong on so many levels but it is done, over and over because no one knows about it, until now. I want to prevent this from happening to any other family. I want to bring these facts to the light.

CHAPTER TWO

"Our world is not divided by race, color, gender, or religion. Our world is divided into wise people and fools. And fools divide themselves by race, color, gender, or religion."
- Unknown

ACTION. I lost count of how many times this chapter was re-written because quite frankly, there's so much to unpack and I didn't know where to even begin. After much contemplation I decided to share one of the most coveted secrets which was the most disturbing and shocking information that I learned about prosecutors during my search for answers. Well, at least for me it was shocking for me. The secret that I unraveled was sickening and made me physically ill and I felt weak in the knees for days as I cried puddles laying in bed balled up in a fetal position for three years.

I won't keep you in suspense so without further adieu, the secret that lawyers don't want us to know is that they make a decision, a judgment about a case -- about you, about me, about us -- and without knowing all of the facts they form an opinion about the case then build a defense based on their biased opinion. It doesn't matter what the truth is or later discovered to be the truth -- the truth is ignored and buried because the man or woman playing God with someone's life has already made the decision on how they plan to proceed with a case and that's that. Even if and despite any evidence to prove the accused man or accused woman is innocent, the truth be damned.

How did we as a collective society allow this to be our justice system? The answer is actually hidden in plain sight: over time, a pay-for-play system emerged and only the special few have access to backdoor deals and the rest of society is cursed for being on the wrong side of the door.

The court system is run by professional programmers who specialize in programming your subconscious because the subconscious mind learns by repetition and not by logic. This is why you can convince someone to believe in something by repeating your argument again and again rather than using logic.

It is known as the psychology of convincing or the law of suggestion which was used by Hitler. Psychology is a terrible weapon in the hands of evil people and Hitler's remarkable understanding of the law of suggestion is how he rose to power.

Every day the Germans were bombarded with propaganda of being an elite race on a daily basis until they began to believe it as the truth. This is an oversimplification of how millions of Germans succumbed to mass thinking in one word: Repetition. Repetition leads to belief.

As a society, as a whole community, as a family, as a nation, we are aware that millions of innocent men and women are wrongly charged, are wrongly convicted or are wrongly committed -- as in the case with my own daughter, on a daily basis. The countless examples of people being railroaded and overcharged and given lengthy sentences is well past acceptability where too many innocent people who are traumatized and altered forever, have become the norm. So the question is *how did we get here?* Repetition makes us turn a blind eye -- especially if it doesn't sit on our own doorsteps and then too many people exist in survival mode where self-preservation is ten times stronger to even care about doing any critical thinking.

I don't know about you, but there's nothing normal about any of this. But despite the biggest legal secret revealed here, there's actually a second secret that's very damning for them but helpful to people who want to advocate for change. As a matter of fact, I'll ratchet this second secret to the top position due it's revelation can begin to change things quite speedily to turn the tide in our favor in the current so-called "legal system" who wins cases by and through character assassination.

CHAPTER THREE
"Strong people don't put others down… They lift them up."
- Michael P. Watson

SETUP FOR THE COMEBACK. There's no easy way to share information that can cut both ways. Another interesting "secret" that I discovered when my daughter's case was thrust into the limelight is a masterclass straight out of Hitler's toolkit because it is yet another strategy from the psychology of things.

Imagine taking prescription drugs that were legally prescribed to you, suffering from an adverse drug reaction from those prescription drugs causing you to become uncharacteristically deluded and violent, and being charged with committing a criminal offense during that state of delusion? This may be difficult to imagine but it happens all of the time. And the reason it is difficult for you imagine is for the following two reasons:

(1) The patient and family members are in shock in the worst kind of way. The mind-numbing events that happen rapid-fire are intentionally orchestrated to overwhelm the family, who are devastated and confused.
(2) The prosecutors count on the family's confusion, and take advantage of it. Wendy Alexander, a prosecutor in Virginia Beach, sent her carefully crafted narrative about the events to the media with the intention to vilify my daughter, and so it began. The court of public opinion was manipulated into supporting a manufactured story.

Now imagine if everyone were on the same level playing field and the truth mattered. My primary goal is to reveal the spark of power inside of you. But in the modern-day carnival of greed, the liars rule the world and they elect to sell us to the highest bidder for their own self-interest. The legal professionals exploited our natural instinct to fear what we do not understand. It is why the BAR Association campaigned successfully to remove civics from the classrooms to eliminate knowledge from our education system. The goal is to keep people ignorant, powerless and distracted with entertainment to the point of total avoidance of our own legal affairs unless the discussion is about hiring an attorney. Then when you hire them, they allow the deliberate manipulation of common activities in the course of life and events, to be painted as "narcissistic" just for the win.

From the moment my daughter's name was vilified in the media, I knew it wasn't going to be easy, but I didn't know that it was going to be extremely unfair. Not once was the prescription drugs mentioned. This was a case of being baptized by fire. I asked Detective Timothy Jones how was it even possible for the media to know anything about my daughter, "The prosecutor told them", he replied. I honestly didn't know how the legal system worked and I quickly realized that my blind faith in the truth coming to light was not going to take place.

More questions. More confusion. More pain. Neither side of the fence was willing to tell the truth. In the glowing interview that praised Annette Miller as a "friend to the mentally ill" she stated that she was going to defend her client to the best of her ability however in most cases where the NGRI (Not Guilty by Reason of Insanity) defense prevails, the client is committed to a hospital longer than if they would have received a 'Guilty' verdict. I didn't know it then but later realized it was a clue by the manner she mishandled the case. Pure, unadulterated Dereliction of Duty, Standard of Care and flagrant Ineffective Assistance of Counsel quite literally flaunted in my face as she chuckled with the prosecutor while staring at me in the courtroom. They behave this way because they know that we are ignorant of the law.

The prosecutor and public defenders are co-workers who make deals that are self-serving to their careers instead of making decisions about the people they are supposed to serve and protect. In fact, Annette Miller didn't object when Wendy Alexander executed the textbook definition of "grandstanding" by waving a stack of papers in the courtroom and referring to the papers as a "50-page manifesto that the defendant wrote to her husband…". However, the court records had copies of 8 to 12 letters as indicated by the different dates in the heading of each letter. Annette had to have known about this grand gesture but she allowed it to be entered as evidence. Blatantly false evidence was allowed. I just continued to wonder when the truth was going to be revealed.

Public defender Annette Miller has a framed copy of the article where the reporter referred to her as "a friend to the mentally ill". However, Annette Miller lies to her clients and ignores them until the last possible moment before a court appearance. I kept the emails from Annette assuring me and my daughter about the list of witnesses who were subpoenaed. But the truth is the witnesses were not subpoenaed and they weren't on the list in the court file. When my daughter and I questioned Annette about the witnesses, we were treated with disdain, dismissed and ignored.

Annette responded to the mental health advocate I hired named David Carmicheal. David is a survivor of the same legal witch hunt that was similar to my daughter's but David's case was in Canada. I found David in a support group on Facebook and I offered to pay him to help my family to advocate for my daughter.

After the money dried out, David quickly stopped communicating with me. By then I had given David $6,000 to cover travel expenses and his outreach efforts to get medical professionals interested in my daughter's case who he claimed would listen to him. I was saddened and disappointed because I believed that David genuinely cared to help my daughter. But as it turned out, during the time that David dropped me, he had recruited another woman named Kristina to visit my daughter at the state hospital to demonstrate his advocacy.

Kristina got in touch with me when she found my email address in a string of messages she received from David. Kristina shared that after visiting my daughter with David, she had given David $19,000 to further his advocacy work. David pretended to be in good standing with a psychiatrist turned advocate to con families into believing he was helping them and to my best knowledge, I believe he is still running the game on other unsuspecting family members who he meets in the SSRI support groups in the name of helping them. There's a special place in hell for him. And more importantly, I have every email between myself and David and everybody else for that matter. I've learned very quickly to only make claims that I can prove and have the evidence to back it up.

CHAPTER FOUR
"She overcame everything that was meant to destroy her."
— Sylvester McNutt III

HARD TIMES. I am far from being "perfect" and I make it a point to never judge anyone, including Wendy Alexander and Annette Miller, because I don't know what goes into their decision making process. However, I could never do 99.99% of the things that they did to my daughter during this nightmare. It is a tale as old as time: People who are in positions of power, develop a god-like superiority complex. Then the added "qualified immunity" enjoyed by prosecutors makes matters worse. They will do everything in their arsenal to keep their authority to the point of obnoxious abuse because it is unchallenged by their victims and their co-workers and cohorts in the legal system. They cover up their violative actions for each other or they look the other way because no one wants to be the one to rock the boat. I don't know how they can sleep at night.

In the case of the "Central Park 5" where 5 teenagers were charged and convicted of sexually assaulting a woman jogger, and later exonerated, one of the men stated *"I was locked up in an institution but I didn't become institutionalized in my mind because I was innocent"*. Their case hit me differently for two reasons: I have a son, and my daughter's behavior was changing from a kind loving spirit to an institutionalized woman in survivor-mode -- forced to be a "model patient" because fighting the system was a heavy burden to bear.

When I hired David Carmichael to help advocate for my daughter, it was because he is only one of the 25,000 cases who realized that to get out of the hospital he had to talk to the media after he was denied a release every year for 5 consecutive years despite being a "model patient". David revealed that the professionals on his team at the hospital were working against him behind the scenes and warned us that it was most likely a part of the "witch hunt" gathering anything to keep patients for as long as possible; reasons that have nothing to do with the patient's progress or level of compliance. As if his words were a well written script, those words became my daughter's reality. Every year, for 5 years, she was transported in a prison van and handcuffed and chained linked inside a cage to the courthouse for an annual review. *Wasn't this excessive security for a model patient who had received a verdict of Not Guilty by Reason of Insanity? And why on earth was the criminal case still open? Again, the verdict was Not Guilty By Reason of Insanity which means the criminal part of the case ended in a verdict and now she should have been on the medical side, where the medical professionals can determine her release, right?* It didn't make sense to me. This is a clear example of INNOCENT IN CHAINS done under cover of secrecy, away from the public eye.

Judge Lilley denied requests for my daughter's release for the following reasons: his lack of understanding about the NGRI protocol, his lack of opportunity to review the files, and so it went for five hearings. Deny. Deny. Deny. Despite a number of medical professionals who testified that my daughter, who they described as the young woman who they interacted with on a daily basis, should be released -- but just one objection from the prosecutor was enough to cast doubt and Judge Lilley would deny the release for another year. During every annual hearing, the prosecutor would conduct a full criminal trial and force my daughter to relive the trauma of being heavily intoxicated by the prescription drugs that caused her to act out of character. The subsequent denial of release would have nothing to do with my daughter's conduct or failure to comply with any of the conditions placed upon her. Just another technicality that would cost her another 12 months of her life because it was of no consequence to them.

I remember that Wendy Alexander must have been disappointed when she went digging for dirt on me. At the time, I was a PhD candidate knee deep to a grasshopper in research for yet another paper while juggling my small website design business, raising a young boy without his father (this papa is the real rolling stone) and working toward my promotion from First Class Petty Officer (E6) to Chief Petty Officer (E7) in the U.S. Navy. But the worst she could claim about me in court was *"the defendant's mother is hanging out on Facebook while her daughter is on trial for attempted murder."* Only in America can a mother be attacked for being a mother. How is this okay? Do I need permission to breathe too? This can't be right. This has to change. I ended my military career and waited two years for my discharge paperwork to process - honorable discharge. Awesome. Thanks. My business folded due to neglect so I lost my house to foreclosure and my ML350 was repossessed by the bank. All good. Too heartbroken to care. In the midst of the worst storm, I gathered a few bits and scraps of courage to begin pursuing legal research.

Despite knowing my daughter was innocent, my ex-son-in-law made the decision to divorce my daughter. This decision prolonged her suffering tremendously. I learned this after discovering a few stories of other women who were facing similar charges and had a supportive husband, the women either weren't charged or faced less punishment. It still bothers me that this man was forced to tell the truth in my daughter's criminal case where he testified that his wife began exhibiting strange behaviors that were uncharacteristic of her normal personality as a kind loving wife and mother. However in the custody matter, his testimony was extremely negative about her. In the beginning, we were still in a state of confusion about what happened and he agreed with me that media interviews would help to clear my daughter's name. It is because of those media interviews, he was prevented from lying about her true personality in the criminal matter. But the family court is closed to the media so he literally relied on lying as his defense. It was shocking to say the least.

This is a man who I welcomed in my home for two years completely rent-free so that they could save up enough money to move out on their own. Although he made the decision to send the children to live with me in Maryland during the 18 months of my daughter's incarceration, he rarely kept in contact with me or with my daughter. In fact, his next door neighbor informed me that he seemed to appear "drunk and high a few times." However, in court he professed to be a good provider who was in constant contact with his children. The court had assigned a guardian ad litem for the children named Carla Kithcart. Carla was biased against me from day one and she snarled at me when I attended my interview with her. She was loud enough for her voice to carry into the waiting room. My attorney, Jennifer Fuschetti, informed me that "everyone is operating as if the mother [my daughter] is guilty so it's going to be difficult for you to win them over".

By this time, my grandchildren were living with me for a year, they were doing well in school and attended weekly appointments with a therapist. Carla Kithcart recommended their father be granted custody despite the fact that he failed her Parental Capacity Evaluation due to "obvious fabrication in an attempt to pass". I passed her mandatory therapy with a clean bill of health. Even the elementary school principal where the children attended school provided an amazing report on how much care, involvement and overall care that went into the children from me. The children's therapist recommended for them to remain with me for the love and stability they would continue to receive. When Fe'licia Holley spoke to the children's father, she expressed her concerns about him being too unstable to Carla. I passed everything she required of me. Dad failed at everything. But none of that mattered to Carla. Carla went along with the program to operate as if the mother was guilty and that was that.

Anyone who disregards the welfare of innocent children in such a nonchalant manner makes that person a special kind of evil. She refused to visit my home and the proposed home of the father because "nobody is paying me to travel to Maryland where the grandmother lives or to North Carolina where the father relocated." I was granted visitation and upon my first trip, I reported the deplorable living conditions to my lawyer, which included no running water in a house directly across the street from an exposed power plant, and a neighbor who saw the children with me reported that the children are seen running around outside unsupervised while their father was working inside the fish warehouse. By the way, this is the fish warehouse that he reported to the CPS Agent named Dawn Hinton that he was going to have a normal work schedule to allow him to care for the children.

The truth fell on deaf ears. They already decided that it was easier to participate in the lie than to go against the popular opinion by telling the truth. They didn't care and they didn't want to help. Even their normally friendly therapist who I was counting on to show compassion toward the children, wasn't willing to help. I will never forget her name. Her name is Fe'licia Holley. She was aware that the children's father told the children that their mother was dead and she simply turned a blind eye because it wasn't her family.

The major players all turned a blind eye to the truth before, during and after my daughter's criminal trial. During the family court trial to determine if the children should stay with me, the woman who was assigned as the guardian ad litem for my daughter, Devon Paige, made very blank statements because she clearly had joined the consensus to operate as if my daughter was going to be found guilty in her upcoming criminal trial. Devon stated to Judge Tanya Bullock "Your honor, I know that I don't have a dog in this race but I am not available on that day." It was sickening to hear a woman referring to another woman, a human being as "a dog" and the most disturbing part is that no one batted an eyelash because it was accepted as perfectly acceptable in open court.

When I lost custody of my grandchildren, I had mixed feelings. On one hand, I was hoping their father would actually love and appreciate them as the gifts they are. On the other hand, I was devastated because I knew that he wouldn't care for them. I knew it was all a show from him just to win at all costs. By this point, the evidence painted a clear picture that he would be unfit to care for two young children on his own because during their entire marriage, his wife was the primary caregiver. Other shocking news about him was when Jennifer told me that she received a report from the plaintiff's therapist that indicated that the man known as his father, was actually his step-father, which was also news to my daughter.

The step-father had actually become quite friendly with Wendy Alexander, the prosecutor in my daughter's criminal case. We learned that he had submitted a negative letter to Wendy from Annette Miller, but our repeated requests to receive a copy of the letter were ignored.

By the time the custody hearing date arrived, I was on the third lawyer and $40,000 into the case. I wondered why Jennifer Fuschetti didn't object when the judge indicated some biased behavior against me. But now that I learned that they operate in tandem as co-workers and the unwritten rule is that all of the legal professionals must fall in line with the undercurrent of guilt towards me simply for being my daughter's mother. Jennifer told me that she didn't understand why Judge Bullock would deny every routine, most basic of requests she submitted on my behalf while granting the vast majority of the plaintiff's requests. It wasn't good lawyering from his lawyer. It was a matter of being found guilty by association before my daughter's trial.

CHAPTER FIVE

"We must always take sides. Neutrality helps the oppressor, never the victim. Silence encourages the tormentor, never the tormented."
- Elie Wiesel

SHINE A LIGHT. The following are excerpts from a forensic medical examination of my daughter's adverse drug reactions to the prescription drugs in her system that Annette Miller declared was "irrelevant to the case".

> The association between antidepressants and violence has been known since the 80s but it drew public attention only after mass shootings in the United States. Just like medication that can disturb the chemical balance elsewhere in the body - like diarrhea caused by antibiotics - the same can happen at the level of the brain. Due to these disturbances, unwilled emotions and involuntary behaviors can occur. When they are severe, they can be considered as a delirium, a toxic psychosis induced by medication. Like all medications, antidepressants and other psychotropic medication can cause side effects. One of the most feared adverse reactions is violence. In the extreme, this can take the form of suicide or homicide.

> In 2001, 76-year-old David Hawkins, known as a loving father and husband, strangled his 70-year-old wife to whom he was married for 50 years. Judge O'Keefe referred to the "conditio sine qua non" in the following way in his ruling: "The killing was totally out of character for the prisoner, inconsistent with the loving, caring relationship which existed between him and his wife, and with their happy marriage of 50 years, I am satisfied that but for the Zoloft he had taken, he would not have strangled his wife."

> It frequently occurs that physicians do not recognize aggression as a side effect of a drug and interpret the symptoms as an underlying psychiatric disease. Delirium caused by psychoactive medication represents a continuum, with, on one end, diffuse complaints of restlessness, and anxiety and on the other end, a condition of fully developed Akathasia (hyperactive form of delirium) with extreme violence, suicide, and homicide.

Leading up to the offense, the medication prescribed to [NAME REDACTED] consisted of: Ambien, Amitriptyline, Bupropion, Citalopram, Motrin, Lorazepam, Tizanidine hydrochloride, Cyclobenzaprine, and Etonogentrel/ethinyl estradiol. It is unlikely the physician who prescribed this medication warned [NAME REDACTED] and her family properly. Instead of weaning her off or at least consider her worsening condition as a side effect, the health care providers diagnose a Major Depression Disorder and prescribe even more psychotropic medication, basically jeopardizing her health even further and facilitating addiction and it becomes evident that leading up to the offense, [NAME REDACTED] developed a toxic psychosis or akathisia.

To gain a correct view of the influence of medication on the psychiatric symptoms, it is important to take the history into account. [NAME REDACTED] has a limited psychiatric history, with problems that are part of daily life. She deteriorated once she was put on antidepressants and was then prescribed more psychoactive medication. She went into a full blown (toxic) psychotic episode, commits the offenses, stopped the antidepressants, deteriorated again. She then restarted the antidepressants, tapered them off, discontinued the co-medication, and improved. [NAME REDACTED] has currently no sign of a psychiatric illness. The fact that after stopping the antidepressant without tapering off [NAME REDACTED] deteriorated is a known phenomenon described in the DSM under code 995.29 "the Antidepressant Discontinuance Syndrome." The importance of taking drug-drug and drug-gene interactions into account when prescribing medication cannot be over-stressed. If any other medication is added or she falls ill with an infection or suffers other health issues, she might very well start accumulating cyclobenzaprine, which has side effects that could mimic psychiatric symptoms. This could be interpreted as a relapse of a psychiatric disorder instead of an adverse drug reaction. I really think under no circumstances [NAME REDACTED] should take any psychoactive medication, she can not metabolize it. With writing this report, I have no intention of going over the trial again or to find any reason to criticize decisions made in the past. I simply want to inform health care providers about the developments in the field of pharmacogenetics, which can help them in weighing the risk whether or not [NAME REDACTED] is still a danger to herself or the people around her. -S.J.M. Eikenlenboom-Schieveld, MD, Forensic Medical Examiner since 1999

Public Defender Annette Miller asked for "involuntary intoxication" but she did not make an argument for it. Judge Lilley stated, "I can not consider involuntary intoxication because I did not hear an argument for it."

Needless to say, this was extremely upsetting to my daughter. However, what was even more unsettling is years after her trial, my daughter learned that Annette had evidence to argue for involuntary intoxication in the form of a medical report from her own expert witness named Dr. Sugden. Dr. Sugden's report stated in clear terms that his professional opinion was that this was a case of involuntary intoxication.

"[Name redacted] suffered from an involuntary intoxication from her psychiatric and other medications that caused a mental and emotional disturbance in her. Medications do have effects on the mind, brain, and behavior. Intoxication anosognosia is the inability when intoxicated by drugs to recognize the mental and emotional impairment caused by the intoxication. It is not voluntary intoxication since the medications were prescribed by a health care provider and was taken according to the directives or prescription and at approved dosages. Psychiatric drugs have a physical impact on the brain. Because [name redacted] was unaware of the potential for this medication to produce abnormal thought processes and behavior and because it was medically prescribed to her, her condition qualifies as involuntary intoxication. If somebody in authority and in a helping profession says take this medication, then that person has power over the patient and would take that medication. There are also cases of people using antibiotics (Levaquin) or acne medication (Accutane) that have a side effect warning of toxic psychosis. If something as seemingly innocuous as an antibiotic can cause adverse medication side effects, how much are psychiatric drugs more likely to cause similar emotional disasters that are even more frequent and more intensive. The individual's overall capacity for self-awareness can be impaired." - Thomas Sugden, Psy. D., Licensed Clinical Psychologist, Forensic Evaluator

During my daughter's trial, Annette Miller had a golden opportunity to allow Dr. Sugden to give his expert testimony on the stand and to make an argument for involuntary intoxication. Instead, she chose to ask Dr. Sugden questions to which he could only answer "yes" or "no". Not once did she bring to the court's attention what Dr. Sugden stated in his report about involuntary intoxication, or that the psychiatrist my daughter was seeing at the time felt that she was being overmedicated by her primary care physician, as reported by Dr. Sugden. My daughter's psychiatrist, Dr. Leslie Murray, was also on the stand during my daughter's trial and testified that she believed without a shadow of doubt that my daughter was a great mother and deeply loved her children. Unfortunately, my daughter's two biggest allies in the courtroom were not allowed to fully voice their expert opinions, which would have allowed the judge to actually consider a verdict of involuntary intoxication when asked to.

Dr. Peter Breggin, psychiatrist and author of Medication Madness stated, "Medical spellbinding in technical language is intoxication anosognosia, the inability when intoxicated by drugs to recognize the mental and emotional impairment caused by the intoxication. Medication madness is an extreme expression of medication spellbinding leading people to behave in ways that they would otherwise reject as hazardous or wrong. Some feel falsely empowered as they compulsively pursue bizarre, dangerous, and even violent actions. Others feel overwhelmed and inexorably compelled toward despair and suicide. Typically these victims of spellbinding are acting in ways that would ordinarily terrify and appall them."

Despite these findings and standard of care, the following hospital evaluators show a pattern of commitment for people who are stable which is unfair and it needs to stop.

During my daughter's evaluation by Dr. Bell, a psychiatrist employed by Eastern State Hospital, he stated "You seem so normal now so I'm having a hard time with this. I don't understand why you're here but unfortunately it is rare to recommend unconditional release."

Dr. Simpson, a psychiatrist employed by Central State Hospital, stated "I've seen the results of your IQ tests and to say you're an extremely intelligent person would be an understatement. But I don't know how to reconcile the person I'm speaking to today from the person on that day of the tragic event...unfortunately we have to commit you."

I sent a copy of Medication Madness to Dr. Simpson and Dr. Bell. Dr. Simpson became angry with me and Dr. Bell ignored me. The standard for commitment is for persons who are unstable, are taking medications, and require time to become stable by slowly reducing their medication. However, the evaluations are a revolving door where stable people are herded into a mental hospital like cattle. Why are they committing people who are stable when they don't meet the criteria for commitment? What is the hidden agenda? My opinion is there is illegal warehousing due to a profit relationship in collusion with big pharma. But, I'm just a crazy mother fighting for the fair treatment of her daughter, right? Am I supposed to allow my daughter's name to be smeared, libeled and censored? The major players in my daughter's case and my custody case for my grandchildren thought I would be too destroyed and distraught to expose them. Not a chance.

To be clear here, Annette Miller, the public defender, dismissed a medical report that would exonerate her client of all charges. Years later is when I realized that Annette dismissed the report because it didn't line up with her defense that was already decided most likely before she even received my daughter's case. And when that determination is already made, it's final. There is no room for changing directions regardless of the actual and relevant facts. Annette made the decision to argue for *Not Guilty by Reason of Insanity* and not even Jesus himself could change her mind. Otherwise, she would look bad in public and she couldn't have any of that.

Back then, it didn't make any sense to me that if the facts and evidence tell you the true story about what happened, then that should be the foundation of the case. Whenever I asked Annette if she would consider arguing for temporary insanity because that's what happened, she ignored me. I sent her a copy of Medication Madness written by a psychiatrist and experienced legal expert with hundreds of cases that proved her client, my daughter, was not a candidate for a verdict of "Not Guilty by Reason of Insanity" because her client was innocent of all charges. "Innocent" is not the same as "Not Guilty."

The law states that Involuntary Intoxication can excuse what normally would be regarded as a criminal act if;

- The intoxication prevents the defendant from knowing what he or she is doing.
- The defendant can't tell what is wrong or right.
- Leaves the defendant lacking the right state of mind to face conviction.

My daughter met ALL three criteria but her public defender never argued for Involuntary Intoxication. Why? In one of the earliest cases on the topic (intoxication from prescribed medications), Perkins v. United States,14 the Supreme Court stated that if a defendant commits an offense while in a mental state amounting to insanity that was induced by a drug prescribed by a doctor, taken in good faith and in accordance with the prescription, then he is not guilty of the offense. In Perkins, a federal appellate court reversed a conviction of manslaughter when the defendant put forth evidence of delirium caused by chloral hydrate prescribed for nervousness.

In Minneapolis v. Altimus 12, a case cited as initiating the modern defense of involuntary intoxication, the defendant argued that he was not criminally responsible for driving under the influence of diazepam (Valium) because he was not aware of the side effects of intoxication. The Minnesota Supreme Court outlined three requirements for involuntary intoxication with prescribed medications: that the defendant did not know, or have reason to know, of the intoxicating effects of the medication; that the prescribed medication, not an alternate substance, caused the criminal behavior; and that the defendant can establish that insanity was induced by the medication (Ref. 12, p 857).

> *"The business of the journalist is to destroy the truth;*
> *to lie outright; to pervert; to vilify;*
> *to fawn at the feet of Mammon,*
> *and to sell his country*
> *and his race for his daily bread.*
> *You know it and I know it, so what folly*
> *is this toasting an independent press?*
> *We are the tools and vassals*
> *of rich men behind the scenes...*
> *They pull the strings... AND WE DANCE."*
> – John Swinton,
> former chief-of-staff for the New York Times,
> in an address to fellow journalists.

If I can find this supreme court case as a non-attorney or lay person, surely a seasoned attorney can do it too. Absolutely! They have access to networks and resources but they only use them when it benefits the "right" people. For the "wrong" people, they put on a good show in open court with theatrical intrigue and a lot of ten dollar words and interrogate nervous witnesses, but the argument for the case is always decided PRIOR to knowing who the client is going to be. In their sick game where they play judge and ruler over the lives of innocent people, they take turns on who will win the next round. Their career record of wins is all that matters to them.

During the three day criminal trial for my daughter, there were three medical witnesses. Dr. Keenan, a psychologist, was hired by the prosecutor. He didn't interview family, friends, co-workers -- no one except my daughter several months after her delusional state happened. In other words, she was lucice because she was no longer on the mind-altering Rx drugs and hadn't been taking them for months by the time the interview occurred. However, that didn't discourage Dr. Keenan from concluding "she is sane and knows right from wrong today." No shit, Sherlock. How about providing a determination on her state of mind during her delusional state. And do I even have to mention the abject failure of a professional investigation? In order for an examination to be valid, Dr. Keenan needed to interview the people in my daughter's life to include family, friends and co-workers. The shit these people do and get away is absolutely incredible.

The second medical witness was Dr. Sugden, a psychologist. Dr. Sugden researched my daughter's background to include interviewing family, friends, and co-workers. He concluded that my daughter was completely out of her mind from the Rx drugs and had no way of knowing right from wrong at the time of the offense.

"A complete forensic evaluation must include collateral interviews with family, friends and associates of the individual being evaluated. This is standard in practice and it allows the evaluator to form a complete opinion." Dr. Sugden, Psychologist.

The third doctor who testified at trial was the emergency room physician who attended to my daughter a few hours after her husband found her. The E.R. doctor testified that my daughter was delusional and clearly and quite visually "out of her mind".

Judge Lilley concluded that Dr. Keenan, who was hired by the Prosecutor Wendy, drew the wrong conclusion about my daughter. Even when it's popular, wrong is never right and I am grateful that my daughter received favor that day.

Needless to say Annette Miller committed various civil rights violations, the worst being the fact that she never discussed the options with my daughter. Imagine if Annette would have had the decency to actually see us as human beings.

CHAPTER SIX

"Remember: Oppression thrives off isolation. Connection is the only thing that can save you. Your story can help save someone's life. Your silence contributes to someone else's struggle. Speak so we can all be free. Love so we all can be liberated. The moment is now. We need you."
- Yolo Akili

REALITY OF LEGALITY. When I began doing legal research in search of answers, the number of civil rights violations were adding up, well into the 90's. I stopped counting when I reached 100. It became very apparent that the public servants who are trusted to protect us betray our trust as a regular course of business. They operate by fraud, for fraud, to commit more fraud -- and no one is outraged by this.

It was just too painful to think about my daughter being escorted back to a jail cell after receiving a verdict of Not Guilty by Reason of Insanity "to wait for a state bed". I called a minimum of 50 lawyers in an effort to get some resolve. Many of them were shocked and appalled. One lawyer got angry and yelled into the phone with disgust "you mean to tell me that your daughter was placed back into a jail cell as an innocent woman? That's not how we're supposed to do things!" During one of my searches to call another lawyer, I found an article about Senator Creigh Deeds, whose son had a violent outburst due to prescription drugs. When the family arrived at the emergency room, they were turned away. I contacted Senator Deeds and continued to call his office every day for three weeks until he agreed to intervene. Within a few days, I received a phone call from the state hospital that my daughter would be transferred from the jail to the hospital the following Monday. When my daughter arrived at the state hospital, the long corridor where she walked past had empty beds.

My daughter and grandchildren were the victims of circumstances. Failed by the system. I researched everyday, eager to find a way to understand what happened to my family. I was going through thousands of legal briefs, videos, articles, anything for clues to unravel the mountain of lies that were told about my daughter. I knew that *one grain of truth could topple a mountain of lies* so I promised myself to keep searching. During the early days of research, I joined a lot of support groups to be surrounded by like-minded people. I quickly learned that most of the group members were charlatans with the intention to sell their garbage legal theories that were fringe to the law. I was easy prey who fell for the act from a few people who could probably sell snow to an eskimo.

One man by the name of Aubrey Harper enjoyed berating people who didn't measure up to his superior intellect. He assured me that he could show me how to have the children returned to me due to the numerous violations. Aubrey wasn't wrong about the violations being brought to light. However, he wasn't kind and he demanded for me to provide him with my email login so that he could send out messages on my behalf. I refused. He refused to refund my $5,000 and referred to it as "a stupid tax" to learn. I felt defeated, but not by the incident with Aubrey. I actually feel sorry for him and for people like him who live their lives taking advantage of people because karma's a bitch who remembers everything.

*"Remember back in the day when parents
would teach their children not to
bully, judge, shame or pressure
their peers or give into peer pressure?
Just because you're in adulthood
doesn't mean your childhood
teachings don't apply.
I am here to connect the disconnected,
the dismembered and the suffering
back to their authentic power and expression."*
- Dr. Raymond Nichols

For me it's not a matter of fair or unfair. It boils down to good versus evil. The golden rule I operate from is *"Do unto others as I would have others to do unto me."* The golden rule the wrongdoers operate from is *"He who has the gold rules."* But if you do things to other people that you wouldn't want done to you or to your loved ones, doesn't that align with the definition of evil? In my humble opinion, all wrongdoers eventually receive a visit from karma without any further thought or intervention on my part so I leave it to the universe. The defeatus feeling that I was experiencing was aimed toward the whole sordid system.

*"The media's the most powerful entity on earth.
They have the power to make the innocent guilty and to make
the guilty innocent, and that's power.
Because they control the minds of the masses."*
— Malcolm X

Most of us are aware that corruption is ripe and rampant in the court system. But unless tragedy strikes close to home, most people are too busy surviving on a day to day basis. And those who are harmed by the justice system are traumatized and distraught as is the case with my daughter. She's one in millions of people who found the strength to survive despite the odds that were stacked against them.

But the truth is forever. With the truth on your side, you win. When you're ready, you'll be the next generation of gladiators who rise to the occasion to remove the old gladiators who come to rob, steal and destroy our personal and collective freedoms.

To every survivor of legal abuse, I say it loud: WHAT HAPPENED TO YOU IS NOT YOUR FAULT. YOU HAVE THE RIGHT TO TELL YOUR STORY ON YOUR OWN TIME, WHENEVER YOU'RE READY. IT IS YOUR STORY TO TELL. WHEN YOU TELL YOUR STORY, IT WILL EXPOSE THE WRONGDOERS. I know you're still healing from the trauma. AGAIN I SAY it is not your fault. You're not naive, you're not a pushover and you're not stupid. You are a normal, kind, considerate human being who was preyed upon by evil dressed in legal titles.

The vast majority of legal abuse survivors are traumatized for life. We have a lot of unresolved feelings from the trauma and struggle with overwhelming feelings of guilt and shame that were projected onto them by the prosecutor and the entire case in general. How did we allow this way of life to become the "norm" in a civilized society? Millions of lives are traumatized by someone who is not held accountable and we just go on vacation? What ever happened to *"presumed innocent until proven guilty"?* The sad truth is that most people ignore the problem until it happens to them or to someone they care about. When I found hundreds of other cases of NGRI where the vast majority ended in a guilty verdict and were sent to prison, my heart sank. This is how I found the book titled "I Am Not Silent" written by Gail Smidkuntz, a distraught father whose son was sentenced to prison. Zach was prescribed antidepressants and soon after experienced Akathisia.

> *Akathisia is an extremely distressing neurological disorder characterized by severe agitation, an inability to remain still, and an overwhelming sense of terror. It is well known to cause suicide. Additionally, akathisia can cause aggression with violent and homicidal impulses, and is suspected to have played a role in certain mass shootings.* (Lucire, Crotty, 2011; Spingola, 2015) [1,2].

Let me be clear, Akathisia is not well known because it is yet another truth that is intentionally buried -- hidden in plain sight from the main stream society and it is certainly never mentioned during the character assassination process by the prosecutors. During a search for answers, Gail found a document titled the "Prosecutor's Manual" by the pharmaceutical company of the drug Zach was prescribed, on how the prosecutor can vilify his son Zach during Zach's trial. The people Zach's life knew him as a "gentle giant" at the youth camp where he worked. He was a kind, lovable, friendly helper and the children loved him. Again, I ask you, how did we get here? How did the deplorable treatment of Zach and countless people become acceptable?

In today's society, being a woman has turned into an extreme sport you'd see in the *Hunger Games*. I'm ashamed to live in a world where life isn't sacred, women aren't cherished and children are stripped of their innocence. I take solace in finding stories of where perseverance ended in triumph. I'll share some of the most encouraging stories of people who wouldn't be defeated no matter what they faced. I celebrate their wins as if it is my win because I feel connected to their soul and I love their indomitable spirit that refused to let go.

People who suffer from mental illness -- whether it is brought on by prescription drugs or not, need medical attention, not jail. *"It's an illness. Do we punish people with any other illness? The comparison has been made this way: a truck driver has a heart-attack and kills 10 people. Is the truck driver a criminal?"* - John Kastner

John Kastner was a brilliant filmmaker and four-time Emmy award winner who was passionate about shining a light on the injustices suffered by mental health survivors who were abused by the justice system. When I contacted John about my daughter's case, he was eager to get the ball rolling. Unfortunately, my daughter wasn't. He had no choice but to move on to the next case to work with someone who was willing to tell their story. He was a kind man who was a bright lighthouse in a sea of darkness.

Dr. Caroline Leaf is a communication pathologist and cognitive neuroscientist with a Masters and Ph.D. in Communication Pathology and a BSc in Logopedics, specializing in cognitive and metacognitive neuropsychology. Since the early 1980s, she has researched the mind-brain connection, the nature of mental health, and the formation of memory. She was one of the first in her field to study how the brain can change (neuroplasticity) with directed mind input. She has helped hundreds of thousands of students and adults learn how to use their minds to detox and grow their brains to succeed in every area of their lives, including school and the workplace.

The truth is the reason scientists can't identify a "depression cell" is because it doesn't exist in the body. Depression and all so-called psychiatric "disorders" are not illnesses, they represent a pattern of reaction to trauma. It is your body survival signal telling you to pay attention to something going on around you. This is trauma and it is treatable through changing the pattern. In other words, giving love and compassion would heal the harmful pattern.

To hear from a neuroscientist that the so-called mental illnesses are a neurobiological response to a stressor is powerful. However, big pharma is a $342B industry so it is profitable to label what happens to be a normal human response to trauma, calling it a disease, and treat it with a pill. The entire mental health profession is controlled and dictated by the for-profit pharmaceutical executives to create the problem and the solution. Big pharma has deep pockets to make damn sure they're profits are protected at all costs, including making sure their products are never named in legal cases. The unholy matrimony between big pharma and our legal system is a known secret that big media wouldn't dare expose for fear of losing advertising dollars.

Here's some sobering facts and statistics. America is one of two countries to allow direct-to-consumer advertising of prescription drugs. Next, America represents only 5% of the world population but has 40% of the world's population in the American prison system. The American criminal justice system holds almost 2.3 million people in 1,719 state prisons, 109 federal prisons, 1,772 juvenile correctional facilities, 3,163 local jails, and 80 Indian Country jails as well as in military prisons, immigration detention facilities, civil commitment centers, and state psychiatric hospitals. It is an American genocide. Sadly, a large percentage are wrongly convicted or committed and experience the most traumatic, unimaginable, vile, inhumane treatment. I don't know how the guards sleep at night. I say, expose the prison guards and everyone all the way back to the arresting police department. When they are exposed and lose pension, the wrongful convictions and wrongful commitments will come to a screeching halt.

Alternatively speaking, Norway's prison system provides homes designed with three core values in mind: normality, humanity and rehabilitation versus the dehumanization of people in the United States. Could this be the answer to reduce recidivism?

Former attorney Katherine Hine submitted a powerful letter of resignation in Ohio, citing it is a private, for-profit corporate system that condones pedophilia, denies recovery of compensation for those whose lives are shattered by the well-connected who help trade in on the churning of controversy via CRIS (Court Registry Investment System) among a multiple of frauds that supports preying on the old, the young, and the disenfranchised of all races and genders.

The reality of legality is that something that is "Legal" doesn't mean "right". "Legal" is the popular opinion at the time. Remember that slavery used to be "legal" and interracial marrieges used to be "illegal". Jail and prisons are modern day slavery. They do not rehabilitate anyone. They cause people to suffer. When people are locked up in cages and treated like animals, you get animals. The Swedish people have the lowest rate of recidivism so they must be doing something right. It is because they treat crime as a dis-ease and focus on getting rid of the problem, not the person.

Rogue prosecutors who manipulate mainstream media to launch their character assassination campaigns to sway public opinion need to be punished in the same manner: exposed and tried in the court of public opinion. Let's see how they like how it feels to expose the vile and reprehensible acts they commit with the facts and evidence to back it up. Their crimes are hidden from public view because it is happening inside the courtrooms and they only share the parts of the story that support their argument(s). Why do you think there is always a sign in the courtrooms warning that "No recording or video devices permitted beyond this point in a State so-called court"? I'll tell you why: You are not in a court of law. You are in a private administrative tribunal of admiralty and statutory equity. Your common law rights must be aligned with the constitutional court of law. However, the court is overrun with deceptive practices, half-truths, unclean hands, denials of due process of law or the assurance of fair and equal protections under the law.

CHAPTER SEVEN
"If you can only be tall because someone is on their knees then YOU have a serious problem"
- Toni Morrison

INSPIRATION. There is an empowerment that comes with grief. Somehow, some way, and at some point some people can find the strength when they need it most. And somehow they find a way to rise from the pain, instead of allowing it to swallow them.

This chapter is dedicated to my heroes. Not every hero wears a cape. They are the brave women and men who survived some pretty horrific, heinous, and inhumane acts that were committed against them by the people who were supposed to uphold the law and the advocates who fought for their rights. I deeply admire their commitment and tenacity, and I draw strength from their strength, especially from the legal abuse survivors who studied law. It is an honor to provide space to recognize them in this book and this chapter is reserved for this purpose.

Albert Woodfox is a former political prisoner who was held in solitary confinement for 43 years due to false evidence.

Chester Hollman was 21 years old when he was wrongly convicted of murder when the police investigator planted evidence against him. He received a wrongful conviction settlement of $9.8 million dollars shortly after he was released at the age of 49 years old.

Hassan Bennett spent 4,606 days in prison for a homicide and related crimes that he did not commit. Failed by an antiquated criminal justice system, Bennett took his case into his own hands, studied the law, filed his own legal briefs, and – ultimately – represented himself in two trials. On May 6, 2019, a jury found him innocent after just 81-minutes of deliberation.

In 2001, Kenny Waters was wrongfully imprisoned 18 years for a murder. Kenny was finally freed after his sister, who was a former high-school dropout, went to law school to prove his innocence.

Keith Allen Harward, a man who was falsely accused, is free after serving 33 years. *"They weren't looking for the truth. They were looking for a conviction. They need to stop this stuff."*

Jonathan Irons was released more than 20 years after he was wrongly convicted on charges of burglary and assault. Jonathan has insisted that he was not at the scene of the crime and had been misidentified. WNBA star, Maya Moore, met Jonathan through the prison ministry in 2007. Maya gave up her basketball career to advocate for Jonathan's freedom. Jonathan is a free man who is now married to Maya.

CHAPTER EIGHT
"The truth is the ultimate weapon where lies once thrived."
- Anelia Sutton

RESTORING FREEDOM. Love wakes me up everyday because I refuse to allow any circumstances or events to change who I am. It's never too late for a new beginning so it's time for us to focus on solutions and tools for change. Guess who fears media exposure? The wrongdoers who are purveyors of lies. Therefore, the number one tool for truth is publicity.

Throughout years of research, the pattern emerged that the same people who manipulate the media with their concocted stories, are crucified whenever the truth comes out about their abuse of authority. Their greatest fear is that their shenanigans would be exposed. But sadly, most legal abuse survivors were targeted because of their lack of connections and limited resources. They are emotionally spent and wiped out, financially *'broke and broken'* in spirit, beat down by the weight of a system running like a well-oiled machine to keep them down. Broken in spirit by the pain of being painted as a monster in the media. Most legal abuse survivors shrink or would rather avoid the one thing that can help them and the one thing their oppressor is also afraid of --- learning the law and publicity! The truth is available, if you choose to go after it.

It begins with one man or woman that can grow into a nation of knowable people. This is known as the butterfly effect. The "Butterfly effect" is interpreted as small inputs can cause massive outputs. A butterfly flaps its wings in Dubuque and later there is a monsoon in Thailand. It seems crazy, but chaos theory supports the butterfly effect. Little inputs really can cause massive outputs. This is sometimes called the 80/20 Principle. The big outcomes in your life will be determined by many tiny actions. It all begins with one little action. This is particularly effective when people take action in the justice system. There is no shame in being a beginner. Just start from where you are then take the next step and go from there.

When there are enough people who take on the mantle to learn how to make the law work for them, soon we'll achieve the critical mass.

> Critical Mass is the smallest size or number that something needs to reach before a particular change or development can happen.

I believe that 3,000 people is our critical mass to effectively change our society back into a caring community of people who give a damn about what happens to one another. It is precisely why I focus on empowering people especially people who were targeted and harmed by the wrongdoers. When I first started a study group with 8 people, I had no intentions of growing beyond that number. I simply wanted to share what I was learning on my own journey. But the need is great and by answering the call I feel good knowing that I am playing a small role in helping other people to avoid the snares and pitfalls that could alter their lives forever. After a few years, the course offerings grew into Mission Possible University. People can learn financial literacy and gain access to wealth and legal education to gain access to justice.

Read this amazing testimonial from a man named Dario who found my YouTube channel. I share it in this book, not to brag, but to demonstrate the power of perseverance which is required when you're fighting an uphill battle.

> "This story starts in the year 2019. It was a very tough year but with the help of Anne's knowledge of the legal system and law...2020 has been a much better year for myself and my daughter..I will explain.
>
> December 13, 2020 ...at this time my daughter and I were still making up time missed due to my child's mother throwing every roadblock she could in the way of me seeing my daughter...this took place for four months. We have always lived in Illinois but on Dec 13th...I was in for a surprise. I received an email from my child's mother on the 13th and it stated that she and my child are now RESIDENTS OF ALABAMA! She did this in secret and forced my daughter not to tell me a thing AND she filed for child support and full custody in ALABAMA!...a state that I had never been to, a state that is 800 miles away and a state where I now needed legal help in.
>
> I've never had to deal with the legal system before so I essentially knew nothing about it. Upon reading the email one could only imagine the

range of emotions and shock that came over me. I was engaged in a battle that totally came from the blind side.

Dec 13 was a Friday so I decided to spend as much time with my daughter as possible (I happened to have her when her mother sent the email) because I know in the coming week....I HAD WORK TO DO!! Knowing nothing, I sought after an attorney hoping to get a free consultation. My prayer was answered and I found an attorney willing to give me free advice. Our call lasted no more than 5 minutes, as he was at the courthouse as we spoke. In those 5 minutes, he gave me a sense of direction in which I took advantage of immediately. I drove around the city all day collecting necessary documents, the following day, I was at the courthouse filing my petition. The clerks were very kind to me and I ended up with an emergency court hearing 3 days later. Now I had every box checked except one...actually knowing what to say and how to say it in open court. I've heard about pro se litigants being eaten alive in court due to ignorance of the law and having no attorney. To say the least I am worried and not just the regular worried....I'm talking about not sleeping or eating right worried ...I'm talking about my daughter, my pride and joy being removed 800 miles away from me!! To say the least, there was much at stake. In ways, I was thankful for that worry because it created a sense of desperation and when humans are desperate, they tend to explore avenues they normally would not...everyone has to feel that. So, as fate would have it, after hours and hours of trying to pick up any information I could while passing up YouTube alleged legal experts charging ridiculous amounts of money, I ran into the iron sharpens iron councils YouTube page.

This was the first channel that spoke to my inner man. There is something in us all, if we lead honest lives, that is able to decipher when something is fraudulent or authentic. I KNEW Anne was the real deal, I could just tell.. I know this is vague but I honestly cannot explain how I knew, I just knew what she was saying was correct.

With that being said, my hunch was correct as I researched everything I heard on the chAnelial and it all came back 100%. Watching and learning from the videos on the channel gave me something that only sound knowledge can provide… TRUE CONFIDENCE!!

Fast forwarding: Anne's channel gave me the confidence I needed by teaching me: YOU MUST LEARN THE LAWS OF YOUR CASE!! By applying this principle, I was able to find and recite the statute ilcs 750 46/305(I will never forget) which forced the judge to order my child's mother to MOVE BACK WITHIN 90 DAYS!!!!!

Anne's channel taught me: THE JUDGE IS NOT THE AUTHORITY IN THE COURT ROOM, THE LAW IS!!! By applying this principle I realized that I did not have to convince the judge of anything, all I needed to do was find the law, understand its application and present it in open court. No judge is above the law.

Anne's channel taught me: APPELLATE COURT OPINIONS CONTROL JUDGES!! This showed me I can present a case from a higher court that must be followed or if step one or two fails! I can take this to a higher court and have any decision not based on the law and its application overturned. (The whole courtroom was shocked I even knew what an appellate court opinion was.)

In closing, I am still engaged in court (family court) but with the knowledge Anelia has helped me attain, the judge has grown very very fond of me. He actually told me in open court that I would make a top tier lawyer. He would have been more surprised if I told him all this was gained within 1.5 months study time and watching Anelia's videos. I have saved THOUSANDS of dollars and Anelia taught, all this can be done with will power and without a lawyer. Small fun fact, the Judge told me in open court that he nor 100's of attorneys who came before him knew the statute that I presented.

I want to personally thank Anne for devoting her energy into helping and educating people. I am sure, with knowledge putting out the flames of fear and stress, years have been added to my time on earth. I want to personally thank Anelia and anyone else involved with the council. This chAnelial has truly been an attribute to me and has changed my life for the better. Love, peace and respect to you all." - Dario M.

The video series that Dario watched is on the IRON Sharpens IRON Council Youtube Channel titled "LEGALLY SPEAKING". I recorded 79 videos and they are one-minute lessons available for free. Click the link to go directly to the playlist. You can find the link to the playlist and read more reviews by visiting https://ironsharpensironcouncil.com.

CHAPTER NINE
"I'm not telling you it's going to be easy, I'm telling you it's going to be worth it."
- Art Williams

WAXING POETIC. Why does society come together as one during natural disaster recovery efforts but return to rudeness before and after? Remember in *Independence Day* when Will Smith's character saved the day by flying a jet into the belly of the beast to save mankind from extinction? Yeah, I want that level of working together for the good of all 365 days of the year!

No other species engages in the foolishness of subjugation of one "kind" over another when all have value. Not wolves. Not lions. Cats. Dogs. You won't see a gray cat reject friendship with an orange tabby. And we are supposed to be the smart ones. Sheeesh. I remember reading a story about a man who saved a newborn baby then 30 years later that baby saved the man's life. It's a beautiful story because two people were kind and good to each other. In that story, do you care about the race, color, gender or religion of either man? You shouldn't. What matters is that every life has value.

For people who don't believe we can overcome a toxic world full of rudeness and misogynoir by turning to kindness, well you're welcome to remain in the dog eat dog world. Go on now. But the fact is that love comes naturally while hate has to be taught so I'm hopeful.

One of the biggest challenges in America is that Americans don't know their rights. And as the saying goes, those who don't know their rights, have none. Most of us are aware of the game play so it is your civic duty to learn about your rights. This study is called jurisprudence, which is the commonly accepted interpretation of the law and applied on a daily basis in the present day court system. It defines Unconstitutional Acts.

"The enemy of my enemy is my friend."
- Enemy Mine (1985)

This law can bring us all together. 16 Am Jur 2d, Sec 177 late 2d, Sec 256: The general misconception is that any statute passed by legislators bearing the appearance of law constitutes the law of the land. The U.S. Constitution is the supreme law of the land, and any statute, to be valid, must be in agreement. It is impossible for both the Constitution and a law violating it to be valid; one must prevail. This is succinctly stated as follows: The general rule is that an unconstitutional statute, though having the form and name of law is in reality no law, but is wholly void, and ineffective for any purpose; since it's unconstitutionality dates from the time of it's enactment and not merely from the date of the decision of branding it.

An unconstitutional law, in legal contemplation, is as inoperative as if it had never been passed. Such a statute leaves the question that it purports to settle just as it would have had the statute not been enacted. Since an unconstitutional law is void, the general principles follow that it imposes no duties, confers no rights, creates no office, bestows no power or authority on anyone, affords no protection, and justifies no acts performed under it. A void act cannot be legally consistent with a valid one. An unconstitutional law cannot operate to supersede any existing valid law. Indeed, insofar as a statute runs counter to the fundamental law of the land, it is superseded thereby. No one is bound to obey an unconstitutional law and no courts are bound to enforce it. Jon Roland: "Strictly speaking, an unconstitutional statute is not a "law", and should not be called a "law," even if it is sustained by a court, for a finding that a statute or other official act is constitutional does not make it so, or confer any authority to anyone to enforce it. All citizens and legal residents of the United States, by their presence on the territory of the United States, are subject to the militia duty, the duty of the social compact that creates the society, which requires that each, alone and in concert with others, not only obey the Constitution and constitutional official acts, but help enforce them, if necessary, at the risk of one's life.

"Any unconstitutional act of an official will at least be a violation of the oath of that official to execute the duties of his office, and therefore grounds for his removal from office. No official immunity or privileges of rank or position survive the commission of unlawful acts. If it violates the rights of individuals, it is also likely to be a crime, and the militia duty obligates anyone aware of such a violation to investigate it, gather evidence for a prosecution, make an arrest, and if necessary, seek an indictment from a grand jury, and if one is obtained, prosecute the offender in a court of law."

This should elicit two fundamental questions now that you are aware about the constitutional violations which have become a standard practice. The first issue should be the obvious and malicious way in which the fundamental rights of American people are being demolished by the court system. The second issue is once you realize that your rights are constantly being violated you have to make a decision on what you are willing to do about it.

> *"Although a lawyer has a distinct advantage*
> *when it comes to dealing with the courts,*
> *no one is to assume that a law degree*
> *created a brilliant mind when*
> *it was actually experience -*
> *which is a great teacher*
> *that is accessible to every*
> *determined man and woman."*
> - Anelia Sutton

WHY SOCIAL MOVEMENTS DON'T WORK. Even the largest movements such as #MeToo and #BLM began with good intentions, but later became hijacked and highly politicized organizations used to pander. I will never forget when I purchased a social media service from a so-called "black man" named @remixreek who did not deliver his services, did not provide my refund and actually blocked me simply for requesting an update about my refund. This so-called "black man" regularly shared that he likes helping people along with #BLM. Ironically, I wanted to support his small business. I texted "Do I matter"? No response. I don't know who hurt him, but he is a small example of people who are comfortable being fake in public, but privately will treat people with extreme disrespect, especially if they believe no one will ever find out. It's such a disappointment, but it displays how bad things are in society where people without a moral compass severely lack empathy.

But the most prominent failure and utter disgrace that stems from the movements is the failure to help the crisis for which they are founded. Truth be told, most movements such as #BLM collects billions in donations but they have a ZERO success rate. It is because the same people who sell the solution, sell the problem. This is not real change, people. It is a financially lucrative business strategy to profit from sensationalism.

In sharp contrast, if the organizations were sincere about improving social justice or any other social plight, then all diseases plaguing modern society would be resolved within 10 years and that would result in 90% of societal issues no longer existing.

"Mahatma Gandhi freed an entire country in 42 years!
Nelson Mandela ended apartheid and unified people in 30 years!
Martin Luther King, Jr. made the world a better place in 10 years!
I believe the world can return to love and light in 5 years!"
- Anelia Sutton

CHAPTER TEN
"The measure of society is how it treats the weakest members"
- Thomas Jefferson

SUCCESS LEAVE CLUES. Knowing your human rights is the best way to stop 99% of the erosion of your rights and the "loss of life, liberty and the pursuit of happiness" through legal contracts. But most people aren't aware of this and waste valuable time arguing about irrelevant facts in court. Remember that no one is above the law and everyone has to follow the rules of the court. You can win every time if you stay focused, remain peaceful, and pursue justice even when the truth is inconvenient for the wrongdoers and their allies. Keep in mind they have very little conscience about condemning innocent people and the truth is irrelevant and inconvenient to them. Forgive them, but proceed as a peaceful woman or man. Relief for active cases and post-convictions will follow.

SELF-ADVOCACY MATTERS. It is your fundamental human right to know what is happening in court. After all, the court is convening to make determinations about your life and your future is hanging in the balance. The law is perfect when there's equity. Equity is the great equalizer because it demands fairness and impartiality from all parties. Fairness is missed if the opposing counsel is spewing fancy, ten-dollar words he or she learned in law school just to impress their co-workers or intimidate the woman or man who is unlearned in law. No sir and no ma'am. Equality is the quality of being fair or impartial. That's it. The entire court system works on your ability to "understand".

POST-CONVICTION RELIEF. In a perfect world, we could trust people in the legal profession to be honest. But in reality, we cannot and we must pursue justice despite them. If you were the victim of injustice or know someone who experienced injustice, there are solutions you can pursue to have a wrongful conviction overturned. The appeals process is the request for a formal change of a decision made by a court of law where sui juris or self-litigants (also referred as "pro se") or attorneys can file a motion to introduce strong new evidence to the courts.

There also may be new evidence or advances in technology such as DNA profiling that change the facts in the case. As a matter of fact, the most common strategy for overturning a conviction is by using DNA evidence to disprove a crime that happened before DNA testing was a viable option. The Innocence Project was founded to exonerate women and men wrongfully convicted, and has found more than 300 post-conviction DNA exonerations in the history of the United States.

If all of your opportunities for an appeal have been exhausted -- or were never available to begin with -- and you still believe your trial was clouded by some kind of an injustice or mistake, you may look into filing a writ. A writ is an order from a higher court directing a lower court to take some kind of action, typically filed in extraordinary situations where an appeal isn't an option.

So, while the trial court may not have erred, a writ may be filed if the verdict was based on some other injustice or error beyond its immediate control. For example, if the attorney violated your rights or if the attorney failed to consider a defense that may have changed the outcome of the case, you may petition the higher court, which is often a federal court, to issue a writ.

INEFFECTIVE ASSISTANCE OF COUNSEL. The Supreme Court has held that part of the right to counsel is a right to effective assistance of counsel. Proving that their lawyer was ineffective at trial is a way for women and men to get their convictions overturned, and therefore ineffective assistance is a common habeas corpus claim. To prove ineffective assistance, a woman or man must show (1) that their trial lawyer's performance fell below an "objective standard of reasonableness" and (2) "a reasonable probability that, but for counsel's unprofessional errors, the result of the proceeding would have been different." Strickland v. Washington, 466 U.S. 668 (1984).

WRIT OF HABEAS CORPUS. Filing a writ of Habeas Corpus requires that the woman or man be in-custody and it is filed in the higher court. If you or your loved one were wrongfully convicted and are imprisoned, this is the appropriate writ for you to pursue.

WRIT OF ERROR CORAM NOBIS. The Latin translation of *Coram Nobis* is "the errors before us." The writ of Coram Nobis is filed in a federal court when there is an error not presented on the record in the trial court, and the error may have produced a different judgment at trial. The error of fact must indisputably result from a miscarriage of justice and must be the only remedy left to correct the error after the woman or man petitioning is no longer in custody, where benefit from the writ is to clear their name of a conviction.

INSANITY ACQUITTAL. The challenge for my daughter's case is that the NGRI (Not Guilty by Reason of Insanity) verdict is considered an insanity acquittal, not a conviction. This would classify her as an "insanity acquittee". Not good enough. She is innocent of all charges. Too many people conspired to condemn her. It is my prayer that this book will open the door to clear my daughter's name. An NGRI verdict happens 1% of the time so it is rare. However, the NGRI verdict translates to years of commitment in a state hospital despite being stable, sometimes longer than a guilty verdict. Jody Henry is the first *medication madness* case to receive a straight "Not Guilty" verdict. That case occurred in Phoenix, Arizona in Maricopa County.

Jody' case means there's always hope. The alternative is to know that liars rule the world and choose to bury your head in the sand like an ostrich. No offense to ostrich lovers, but we're better than that. Millions of innocent people are locked in cages. And even when they present irrefutable evidence of their innocence they still have an uphill battle just to prove that they're innocent. I repeat, millions of women and men who are innocent with evidence of their innocence are forced to remain incarcerated while they file motion after motion, which could take many, many years -- just because someone doesn't want to look bad for being wrong. The ego is cruel. It is the most asinine case of bullshit I've ever heard in my life. Doing "nothing" is not a viable option. But it is happening on a daily basis because no one is up for the challenge. Until now. It's time for more good people to get to work. If you stay asleep, you are complicit with the liars and you've agreed to their lies.

IMPORTANT NOTICE. I am a mother and an advocate for justice and truth. I am still learning and still healing. I am not a lawyer, nor do I practice law so none of this is to be taken as legal advice. I will also remind you that a major challenge that anyone can face as an advocate is that every state, county, and court operate differently with different requirements across the board. Then there are the different personalities with their own personal issues, giant egos and god-complex you'll encounter in the so-called halls of justice. Needless to say it is not feasible for me or anyone to know every state, county or court requirement. Please and kindly conduct your own due diligence for accuracy and applicability to your own legal affairs.

CHAPTER ELEVEN
"A free people [claim] their rights as derived from the laws of nature, and not as the gift of their chief magistrate."
- Thomas Jefferson, Rights of British America, 1774

SELF-EDUCATION IS KEY. Eric Glisson spent nearly 18 years in prison before being exonerated. The real killers were the homicide cops who "fabricated evidence and false witness testimony" that convicted Eric and four co-defendants in the fatal shooting of Baithe Diop. There are tens of thousands of stories like Eric's. Lives ruined and most times the corrupt authority gets away with it. Please don't wait until it happens to you or your loved ones. I hope it is enough to know that the problem exists in the first place. Learn how to make the law work for you by learning the law of your case. That's all. That is all. You don't have to learn an encyclopedia of the 5 million laws. Just learn the law of your own case to win. When you're armed with that knowledge, you are well-equipped to help yourself, then you can turn your attention to helping others. When you hear about a story on the news, please question it. Know that there are liars and underlying operators who are hoping for you to jump to the wrong conclusion by dangling a carrot in your face and calling it the truth. Don't fall for it anymore.

ADVOCACY IS SUNLIGHT. Attorneys and judges should be held accountable to the same laws as every woman and man. They shouldn't be allowed to use special privileges to avoid prosecution if they have done something wrong. It is a simple and reasonable request. This simple request was made clear in the case of Hale v. Hale: "The innocent individual who is harmed by an abuse of government authority is assured that he will be compensated for his injury." See Hale v. Hale, 201 US 43, 26 S.Ct.370, 50 L.Ed.652.

Lies exposed to the light of day is a powerful way to restorative justice. The next chapter of my life is to file an amicus curiae brief on the grounds of civil rights violations, human rights violations, perfidy and violations of public trust committed by the attorneys involved with my daughter's case. It is not about revenge, it is about moral duty, ethics and justice.

I have walked through hell and I kept walking. I have paid a heavy price for the experiences that I share in this book to pay it forward so others don't have to learn these lessons the hard way. I have never done anything *just for money*. Money, fame and power don't appear on my list of priorities. As a whistleblower of corruption, I am armed with the truth when the other side retaliates, I smile because I know that "One grain of truth can destroy a mountain of lies" and I'm armed with the truth, only the truth and nothing but the truth, so help me God.

An *amicus curiae* is a friend of the court so I invite all human rights activists and advocates to file an amicus curiae brief in your local courthouses. **An amicus brief can be presented by anyone interested in influencing the outcome of a lawsuit but who is not a party to it. Anyone can intervene in any matter for justice to be served. However, it is important to note that you should always call the court for the rules and procedures.**

AMICUS CURIAE. In the United States, An amicus curiae is a friend of the court. A group is amici, the plural of amicus curiae, is an intervenor, which can be a woman, a man or an organization who requests to provide legal submissions as a relevant alternative or additional perspective regarding the matter(s) in dispute. It is a person with strong interest in or views on the subject matter of an action, but not a party to the action. It may be filed by private women and men or the government to petition the court for permission to file an amicus brief on behalf of a party to suggest a rationale consistent with her or his own views.

It is similar to a *McKenzie Friend*. A McKenzie friend assists a litigant in a court of law in England and Wales, Northern Ireland, the Republic of Ireland, New Zealand, and Australia by quietly giving emotional support, moral support, advice and taking notes without the need for any legal training or professional qualifications. The exception is that Amici addresses the court and a McKenzie Friend addresses the litigant only. I must remind you that the 6th Amendment states "You have the "right to counsel", not an attorney. Counsel means advice. Words matter so please pay attention to them.

AMICUS CURIAE BRIEF. An amicus curiae brief informs the court on points of law that are in doubt, gathers or organizes information, or raises awareness about some aspect of the case that the court might otherwise miss on an active case. The person is usually, but not necessarily, an attorney, and is usually not paid for her or his information. An amicus curiae must not be a party to the case, nor an attorney in the case, but must have some knowledge or perspective that makes her or his views valuable to the court.

An amicus curiae brief is commonly filed in appeals concerning matters of a broad public interest such as civil rights cases. In appeals to the U.S. courts of appeals, an amicus brief may be filed only if accompanied by written consent of all parties, or granted on motion by consent of the court. All readers are highly encouraged to make an inquiry on how to submit an amicus brief in the interest of public safety whenever you come across a case of extreme social injustice.

PERFIDY. The Latin root of perfidy is made up of *per*, or "through," and *fidem*, or "faith" which means "deceitfulness" or "treachery." So it's not just being unkind, but deliberately betraying a trust. So in order for perfidy to happen, there has to have first been a sense of faith in place, which was then broken or betrayed. It is the basis for an amicus brief for the advocate who desires to file on behalf of women and men who were wrongfully convicted and wrongfully committed, as in the case of my daughter and millions of other innocent and sane women and men.

CORRUPTION. Corruption in the courtrooms is out of control. It is no longer an option to wait for injustice to land on your doorstep. You can submit an amicus curiae brief as a preventative, so that it doesn't land on your doorstep. Everytime you submit a brief, you may be saving the life of someone you know and love in the future.

SUI JURIS. Many will tell you that you cannot find justice without an attorney in our broken and corrupt legal system. This is simply not true. As a petitioner in *Sui Juris* you possess a power that is not available to lawyers, which is that your legal paperwork can include the truth supported by evidence. Laypeople are not bound to adhere to the strict rules and procedures of the court in form or function. But in sharp contrast, the primary goal of a legal professional is to maintain their professional relationships and make sure that their professional reputation remains stellar in the court system. Second, far more emphasis is placed on whatever rules and procedures that suit their desired result as long as it is not exposing their co-worker who happens to be opposing counsel who includes the judge, or they risk losing their license to practice law. Despite rampant corruption, it makes no difference to most of them. The legal profession has the unwritten rule and line of demarcation. There are club members and there are non-club members and club members protect the club. You are not a club member. Therefore, the club members will turn a blind eye to the actions by the rotten club members. They don't do things just for the sake of "doing the right thing", not even for all of the tea in China. For example, three lawyers refused to file a motion to recuse a corrupt judge on my behalf. The unspoken rule for them is to turn a blind eye to justice. So expecting them to help you is not gonna happen, captain. Not for me, not for you, not for anyone.

CHAPTER TWELVE
"The only thing necessary for evil to triumph is for good men to do nothing."
- Edmund Burke

HEALING. Millions of people, including myself, suffer from two invisible medical conditions. They are Broken Heart Syndrome and Legal Abuse Syndrome.

Broken heart syndrome is a condition that can cause rapid and reversive heart muscle weakness, also known as stress cardiomyopathy. It is caused by two kinds of stress — emotional or physical. But while most people with this condition experience a stressful event, up to 30% of patients have no identifiable trigger at the time of their initial symptoms. Broken heart syndrome can be life threatening. In some cases, it can cause severe heart muscle weakness. That's the scientific explanation. Let me tell you how it feels. It feels as if there is a tiny scratch on my heart that physically hurts every time I get too down in the dumps. It's not depression. I reject, refuse and vehemently rebuke ANY and ALL psychiatric terminology to be applied to the human condition called "life". But hey, that's just me. Especially now that I know for sure that new psychiatric terms are manufactured then voted on by big pharma for the next iteration of the DSM (Diagnostic and Statistical Manual of Mental Disorders). Conflict of interest, much?

Legal Abuse Syndrome is described as "devastation to prolonged injustice by slander, misinformation, and deception treated as facts", in the book with the same name written by the woman who coined the term. Dr. Karin Huffer conjoins law, therapy, and research revealing a subtype of Post-Traumatic Stress Disorder. "Those who abuse power simply have a new battleground and gun their victims down with paper bullets and words designed to exclude, dehumanize, and annihilate their final hope and last dollar. Instead of justice, these persons with disabilities were impoverished and left with the scars of traumatic stress layered upon their already existing problems."

Legal Abuse Syndrome helps victims through facts, graphics, and heart rendering vignettes to grasp elements of this injury, recognize its causes, and benefit from the therapeutic steps provided as a self-help tool for cumulative trauma. When systems of care, i.e. the judicial system, cause or exacerbate medical conditions due to extreme stress, the dilemma presents a public health problem as well as a multidisciplinary legal/medical professional challenge. *"There is nothing wrong with you. You need a game changer that bolsters your resilience and confidence.*

Eight self-help steps guide you through the toughest times of your litigation illustrated by gripping cases of human courage and principle against the massive power of the judicial system. The people you meet in this book will encourage you. James' case portrays civil court being skewed to cover up a felony while fraud on the court is recklessly used to hide the facts. The issues become twisted into a dizzying "house of mirrors" with lies taking on a life of their own in the courtroom. When rage is exceeded in the human experience, one either explodes or implodes. Explosion usually results in violations of civility and law complicating the problem. Implosion leads to health consequences and bitterness. Legal Abuse Syndrome guides you toward an alternative that allows the victim to skillfully stay in the fight. Along the way, there are gifts in reviving the spirit of justice, a staple of a civilized society."

> "When you control opinion, as corporate America controls opinion in the United States by owning the media, you can make the [many] believe almost anything you want, and you can guide them."
> – Gore Vidal from The Golden Age

TRUTH BE TOLD. Monsters DO NOT live in the dark. They walk among us. They smile in our faces but they relish in the low frequencies known as guilt and shame. This is their weapon of choice because they're aware that your suffering will grow in silence. It takes time to stop courtroom corruption. When you stay silent, they win. And worst yet, you become an ally to the criminals. You are complicit to the crimes they commit against you and others.

The road to recovery is to speak out. Speaking out defeats the monsters because they are afraid of the truth seeing the light of day. But the truth is that 99% of legal survivors don't take any action so the only voices that are heard are from the liars. 90% of society are asleep or don't care enough. 5% know and are trying to wake the 90% but the 1% don't want the 5% to wake the 90%. When we speak up, we transfer power from the 1% to the 99% and only then will we see change

CHAPTER THIRTEEN
"More hands make the work easier."
- Jonathan Irons

COURAGE TO CHANGE. I want to be clear about my intentions on two issues. First, survivors of legal abuse don't owe the rest of society anything. Your survival of the unimaginable horrors is more than enough for me to honor them as heroes. You have the right to say what you want to say, when you want to say it. However, the point of this book is to show you that speaking out can help you to heal as well as help prevent others from suffering through hearing your story. In recognizing the consequences of structural & institutional abuse and systemic oppression of people outside of the legal profession, who demonize innocent people, we should all acknowledge the need for a network of people willing to help expose it to the world. But even if you can't find your voice through sharing your story publicly, I implore you to empower yourself by knowing your rights through self-education. Even when I didn't have the fight in me, becoming acquainted with my rights as a human being has been a great equalizer for me. It is how I began to feel empowered after feeling powerless for far too long.

Second, there are good and bad police and lawyers. They know there's a better way to operate without attacking people in a cruel way. The ones who choose to harm people are the real criminals, and couldn't survive the pain that they inflict on others. There is a history of intimidation of witnesses, suspects, and victims. They do what they do, again and again, because they operate with the belief they will get away with it. They are encouraged and celebrated when they bully their victims -- which include witnesses -- into submission with fear and intimidation tactics that would make Genghis Khan blush. However, when they are exposed, they can not and do not handle any hint of scrutiny of their wrongdoing. That was the case for the exposed prosecutor in the case of the Exonerated Five formerly known as the Central Park Five. That was the case for the prosecutor who handled the case of Isaac Wright, Jr. -- the man who studied law while in prison to eventually win his freedom by exposing the prosecutorial misconduct. They can dish it but they can't take it. But, I don't want anyone to misconstrue my intent as pressure to relive the trauma. My intent is to simply demonstrate that those who speak out found healing from doing so.

MOTIVATION. Haters are going to hate. It is what they do. Let them relish in their job while you focus on your job. What do you want to be remembered for? Lying in bed watching a movie is temporary pleasure. But service to humanity brings an immeasurable serving of delight with a side order of joy. Do you want to be remembered for keeping up with the "cool" kids who exploit people? I refuse to be conditioned into accepting that the behavior from legal professionals is acceptable. It is not and I will not. Not now. Not ever. We have a moral obligation to help each other. So I lifted myself out of wallowing in sorrow and I went to work on legal research.

MINDSET. My love for humanity is perfectly illustrated in the wolf story. One evening, an elderly Cherokee brave told his grandson about a battle that goes on inside people. He said, " My son, the battle is between two wolves inside us all. One is evil. It is anger, envy, jealousy, sorrow, regret, greed, arrogance, self-pity, guilt, resentment, inferiority, lies, false pride, superiority, and ego. The other wolf is good. It is joy, peace, love, hope, serenity, humility, kindness, benevolence, empathy, generosity, truth, compassion and faith." The grandson thought about it for a minute and then asked, "Grandpa, which wolf wins?" The old Cherokee simply replied, "The one that you feed." So, which wolf are you feeding?

POWER UP. If you survived any kind of trauma and you are still a kind and loving woman or man, please know that you are powerful. Then when you combine that power with the power to forgive, you begin to heal yourself because forgiveness isn't just for the one being forgiven. We know that holding on to the low frequencies of negativity is like drinking poison expecting to affect the other person. It doesn't. No one is perfect, so forgive them without judgment. I'm not saying to let them off the hook. Still expose their violations, when you're ready. But the moment I forgave the purveyors of lies in the halls of justice, was the moment I restored my power. They were counting on my demise but I am still here and I am growing stronger day by day. Each day that I survive, I win. I know that I am stronger than those who participate in harming people and who give into the herd mentality and "go along to get along". They are weak. Please forgive them.

THE LION AND THE GAZELLE. "Every morning in Africa, a gazelle wakes up, it knows it must outrun the fastest lion or it will be killed. Every morning in Africa, a lion wakes up. It knows it must run faster than the slowest gazelle, or it will starve. It doesn't matter whether you're the lion or a gazelle - when the sun comes up, you'd better be running." - Christopher McDougall, Born to Run: A Hidden Tribe, Superathletes, and the Greatest Race the World Has Never Seen

Whether you choose to be a gazelle or a lion is of no consequence. It is enough to know that with the rising of the sun, you must run. And you must run faster than you did yesterday or you will die.

I am hopeful for what the future holds for the next generation. But in this moment in time, please love yourself, learn your rights and lose the fear. This is the race for life. Make it count.

Whenever I need a boost of encouragement, I read the following quotes. These quotes can nourish your soul in the midst of the storm, if you let them.

"I believe that everything is a matter of heart. Darkness -- hate, greed, racism -- is taught by hurt people who themselves learned from hurt people. When enough people choose to become the light through small acts of love, peace, generosity and kindness, the future generations will be born into lightness, and can appreciate the contrast of darkness from the pages of our history books."
- Anelia Sutton

"Mahatma Gandhi freed an entire country in 42 years!
Nelson Mandela ended apartheid and unified people in 30 years!
Martin Luther King, Jr. made the world a better place in 10 years!
I believe the world can return to love and light in 5 years!"
- Anelia Sutton

"Share your experiences and you'll grow a culture of kind, educated people."
- Anelia Sutton

"I am grateful for things that bring joy or painful lessons because all experiences offer the opportunity to grow."
-Anelia Sutton

"Truth be told the accused party never has to prove anything. In fact, when the accused attacks the accuser's errors, the case is easily dismissed."
- Anelia Sutton

"Martin Luther King, Jr. said 'Darkness cannot drive out darkness; only light can do that. Hate cannot drive out hate; only love can do that.' I believe that everything is a matter of heart where love is innate without the need for lessons. Darkness, which includes hate, greed, racism, is taught by people who are hurt who learned it from hurt people. But when enough people choose to be the light, through small acts of love, peace, generosity and kindness, the future generations will be born into light, and can appreciate the contrast of darkness from the pages of our history books."
- Anelia Sutton

"To remain silent, is to be complicit with the wrongdoers."
- Anelia Sutton

"If I ruled the world I'd free all my sons."
- Nas & Lauryn Hill

Dear Reader:

The purpose of this book is to be a vehicle for change. If you believe the truth should be the goal in our justice system then I invite you into a Giving Pledge which is to purchase extra copies of my book to give away to people in your own community. The education in this book will help to build a nation of people who are willing to speak up, and advocate like peaceful gladiators for the sake of mankind.

PEACEFUL GLADIATORS. I stand for accountability, not hate. I repeat, I stand for accountability, not hate which is the reason I exposed the names of the wrongdoers. If you are interested in advocating for justice in a peaceful manner, I welcome you with open arms to join the league with me to begin exposing the names of all wrongdoers until they learn to stop doing people wrong.

As a woman or man who desires to fill any free time with civic duty, you can join my free legal study group on my website. When you join, you'll receive free training on how to take back control of the justice system, county by county, state by state. There's no need to march anywhere. No need to shout angry rhetoric. No need to make demands to anyone -- especially politicians. No need to call anyone names or make accusations or accuse anyone of being racist just to pander. None of that will be tolerated. Come with love in your heart or just stay home. Peaceful advocacy is how we roll and how we win. Remember, the pen is mightier than the sword and you attract more bees with honey. All of the successful strategies that endured the test of time were peaceful.

EMPOWERED TO EMPOWER. Giving back to the community is in my DNA. Therefore, a portion of all proceeds goes to the initiatives for social change listed on https://ironsharpensironcouncil.com. So when you invest in yourself, you're also investing in changing the world.

THE CLEAR HER NAME FILM. Every contribution contributes to the making of the film (and new films) to help spread a message of hope through advocacy, which in turn supports all of humanity. To make a contribution, please scroll down to the bottom of the page when you visit https://ironsharpensironcouncil.com.

RECOMMENDED FOR FURTHER ADVOCACY AND SELF-EMPOWERMENT

These resources will provide you with more than enough material to become a legal gladiator. In short, you do not need to hire me (or anyone) and I highly discourage it.

(1) REFERENCE MATERIAL. There is a list of books, films and courses that I highly recommend for your advocacy journey. For the most up-to-date references, please review the references listed on https://clearhername.com/resources.

(2) CLEAR HER NAME COMPANION WORKBOOK. The Clear Her Name book is effective as a stand-alone book. However, the practical tips, tools and templates that are provided in the companion workbook is a great resource for those who are interested in legal research, whereas a combination of the Clear Her Name book and the Clear Her Name Companion Workbook provide you with a strong foundation to begin advocating for yourself and advocate for your family and your community. A portion of the proceeds will go toward the Clear Her Name film project. You can order a copy of the workbook by visiting https://clearhername.com/book.

(3) FREE LEGAL STUDY GROUP. The wrongdoers who break the law use intimidation, and isolation to bully you (or your loved ones) into accepting their unlawful actions. But you are no longer alone. I highly recommend that you join my supportive community. It is a FREE research and study group on Facebook. You may post questions in the group, then pack your patience. The link is found on https://ironsharpensironcouncil.com.

(4) JURISDICTIONARY PERSONAL LEGAL COURSE. I highly recommend that you enroll into the legal course written by Dr. Frederick Graves who I interviewed for my YouTube channel. Dr. Graves is an advocate first, followed by the title of being a retired lawyer after 30 years of experience. He is passionate about teaching people how to navigate the landmines and booby-traps waiting for you in the courthouses. You can find the link to his course on https://ironsharpensironcouncil.com.

(5) DREAM LAW SCHOOL FOR LEGAL ADVOCATES. This is an advanced course for lay people (non-lawyers) who are legal researchers. It is a deep dive into a secret knowledge trust to quickly gain decades of law education in days. Upon graduation and earning a diploma, the graduate can provide counsel to their family and community as a legal gladiator. Includes Student Q&A Forum, Graduate Forum and Monthly Hangout with Anelia Sutton. Save $100K & 4 Years of Law School and $$$Thousands in Legal Fees! You can find the link on https://ironsharpensironcouncil.com.

(6) FINANCIAL EMPOWERMENT. When I began my career as a legal researcher, I noticed a key pattern. The people who are targeted the most, are people who are struggling financially -- the most vulnerable and preyed upon by the legal profession. So the other half of the equation in the

journey for justice is financial empowerment. This self-defense requirement is the website below where you can enroll in several online courses to repair your personal credit scores, start an online business, and build generational wealth. You may also join my free masterclass to access the top three strategies the ultra wealthy elite 1% do, even if you're starting from scratch. You can register for FREE training on https://ironsharpensironcouncil.com.

FINAL THOUGHTS. First of all, thank you for purchasing this book. You could have picked any number of books to read, but you picked this book and for that I am extremely grateful. I hope that I have added value and quality to your everyday life. If so, it would be really kind if you could share an honest review about this book on Facebook, Twitter and Instagram.

I want you, the reader, to know that your review is very important and so, if you'd like to leave a review, all you have to do is find Clear Her Name on Amazon and away you go. If you enjoyed this book and found some benefit in reading this, I hope that you could take some time to post a review on Amazon. Your feedback and support will help make this book even better and to greatly improve my writing skills for future projects.

WRITTEN WITH LOVE FOR HUMANITY. If you're willing to help spread this message, here are some simple ideas to make it happen:

1. Start Your Own Prison Reform Campaign: Send a hard copy of this book to our brothers and sisters who are trapped in the prison industrial complex.

2. Start Your Own Celebrity/Influencer Campaign: Send the Amazon link with #clearhername in an email or comment on social media to your favorite celebrity/influencer who shows an interest in social justice issues.

3. Start Your Own Media Campaign: Send a copy of this book to investigative journalists connected to mass media outlets who show interest in social justice issues.

Thank you, any help will be greatly appreciated and I wish you all the success in your future!

- fin -

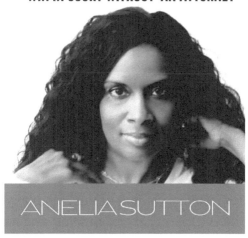

http://clearhername.com/book

The Author

Anelia Carmila Sutton is an American author, advocate and amicus curiae (friend of the court who intervenes for the greater good).

Anelia Sutton is a bestselling author featured in over 240 media outlets and web portals including NBC, ABC, CBS, Fox News, Huffington Post and Forbes. She co-authored *Performance 360* with the world's leading entrepreneurs including Richard Branson under her birth name.

After nearly losing her daughter and grandchildren to Adverse Drug Reaction (ADR), Anelia began advocating for change through her advocacy websites on http://clearhername.com and http://CampaignforJoy.org. Through this mission, Anelia increased ADR awareness, and supported individuals and families who were affected by adverse drug reactions.
Although she walked away from her successful small business to pursue advocacy work, Anelia was once known as the world's highest paid website design consultant.

Anelia Sutton is a United States military veteran of the U.S. Navy with an Honorable Discharge, earned a B.S. in Holistic Nutrition, B.S. in Liberal Studies, and an MBA. Anelia graciously accepted a post-master's certificate offered by the university after completing 45 out of 60 credits in her doctoral studies. She is a member of the National Association of Female Executives, and recipient of America's Premier Experts award.

Anelia resides in Maryland with her son, and her two cats. You can connect with Anelia through her website https://aneliasutton.com.

Made in United States
Troutdale, OR
07/23/2025

33144304R00038